D1521726

laugh

A LOT

YOUR DAILY DOSE OF
WHOLESOME, HEAVENLY HUMOR

TODD & JEDD HAFER

elevate

EDITORIAL
WORK
AnnaMarie McHargue,
Dave Troesh

COVER
Aaron Snethen

INTERIORS
Aaron Snethen

© 2016 by Elevate Publishing

LIBRARY OF CONGRESS
2015956303

ISBN HARDCOVER
9781943425211

ISBN EBOOK
9781943425693

laugh A LOT

YOUR DAILY DOSE OF
WHOLESOME, HEAVENLY HUMOR

TODD & JEDD HAFER

INTRODUCTION

Laughs. We share them, send them, feel them, and seek them. We sing about laughter, talk about it, write about it, dream of it, and even Tweet about it. Sadly, sometimes we can't spare even one laugh.

But the laughs are there for the enjoying. Steve Martin said that a comedian's job is simply "talking about what's going on. And there will always be something going on." This is good news because, of all the gifts life gives us, humor is one of its sweetest. We laugh with our kids, laugh at our pets, and, sometimes, laugh right in the face of danger, fear, or grief. Most of all, we love to laugh with those special people God has placed in our lives. This book celebrates laughter, in all its glory, foibles, and mysteries. In the following pages, you'll find a literary feast of things ridiculous, remarkable, and downright wonderful. We hope this book will help you celebrate the many ways laughter can surprise, delight, amaze, comfort, and enrich life like nothing else on earth.

DID YOU KNOW?

Hundreds of years ago in England, couples who were willing to swear on the King James Bible that they hadn't engaged in a marital spat for an entire year were rewarded with a side of bacon.

TODAY'S QUOTE

"I keep trying to throw away my boomerang. It's darn-near impossible!"

Jedd Hafer

SOMETHING TO PONDER

Why aren't more people– or any people–
named Lazarus these days?

TODAY'S QUOTE

"Do not ask yourself, 'Why can't
I get my ducks in a row?'

Ask instead: 'Why this compulsion
to organize waterfowl?'"

Todd Hafer

BULLETIN BLOOPERS

This afternoon, we will hold congregational meetings in the South and North ends of the church. Children will be baptized at both ends.

At the conclusion of today's service, a special collection will be taken to defray the cost of the new carpet. All those wishing to do something on the carpet should come forward and do so.

Our special music today will be provided by Dale Anderson, DDS. He will be singing "Crown Him with Many Crowns."

Our church will host a potluck dinner tonight, featuring live music. This promises to be a memorable evening for both the young and the young in heat.

The senior choir invites any member of the congregation who enjoys sinning to join us right away!

TODAY'S QUOTE

"I like long walks, especially when they are taken by people who annoy me."

Fred Allen

SIGN FROM GOD

SHAWNEE CHURCH

For God so loved the world that He did **NOT** send a committee.

8
SOMETHING TO PONDER

Noah was a brave man who set sail in a wooden boat that included at least two termites, two woodpeckers, and two beavers as passengers.

9
DID YOU KNOW?

Bela Lugosi, the Hungarian actor who played Dracula on stage and screen, knew almost no English. He learned his lines phonetically, and, early in his career, had little idea what he was saying. Lugosi played Dracula for nearly 30 years, forsaking almost all other roles. He was even buried in his Count Dracula garb.

10
TODAY'S QUOTE

"Here are two things I love about working
on my car in the driveway:

I can do it with my kids.

I can do it without my kids."

George House

11
SIGN FROM GOD

UNITED METHODIST CHURCH
Sign Broken.
Please come inside for message.

12
SEEN ON A BUMPER STICKER

IF YOU'RE LOOKING FOR A SIGN FROM GOD TO GO BACK TO CHURCH, MAYBE THIS IS IT.

13
TODAY'S QUOTE

"The journey of faith is long– better take snacks."

Dan Taylor

BULLETIN BLOOPERS

The peacemaking meeting scheduled for today has been cancelled due to a conflict.

Ladies, remember the rummage sale! It's a chance to get rid of those things not worth keeping around the house. (Don't forget to bring your husbands!)

Our youth basketball team is back in action Friday night at 8 in the Rec Hall. Come out and watch us stomp Sacred Heart of Mary.

Remember next month's Prayer & Fasting conference. Registration is only $50, and that price includes all meals and snacks.

15
TODAY'S QUOTE

"Love is the most important thing in the world, but baseball is pretty good too."

Yogi Berra

BULLETIN BLOOPERS

Due to the Rector's serious illness, Wednesday's healing service has been postponed indefinitely.

Terry Jones will play this Sunday's offertory, "Jesus Paid It All."

We thank our missionaries to Mexico, who spoke very briefly last week– much to the delight of the audience.

Last Sunday's worship service was a smashing success. Special thanks to Jennifer, the pastor's daughter, who volunteered to play the piano, which fell on her, as usual.

Please note: While our pastor is on vacation, massages can be given to the church secretary.

17

Based on recent viewings of Christian cable TV, more and more televangelists are doing their clothes shopping at Winko's Apparel Shop for the Tall and Husky Clown.

TODAY'S QUOTE

"I'm not denyin' that women are foolish; God Almighty made 'em to match men."

George Eliot

SEEN ON A BUMPER STICKER

FORBIDDEN FRUIT CREATES MANY JAMS!

20
THE CHRISTIAN AND THE LION

One day in ancient Rome, a lion chased a Christian through the streets. Soon, it became obvious to the exhausted man that the lion was going to catch him. So he turned suddenly, dropped to his knees, and prayed, "Lord, please make this lion a Christian like me!" Instantly, the lion kneeled too. He folded his forepaws and prayed, "Dear Lord, for this meal of which I am about to partake . . ."

BULLETIN BLOOPERS

The 8th-graders will be presenting Shake-speare's "Hamlet" in the church basement at 7 p.m. this Friday. The entire congregation is invited to attend this tragedy.

Next Sunday afternoon, Farmer Jones will host our youth, giving them a behind-the-scenes tour of his diary.

Our Low Self-Esteem Support Group will meet Thursday at 6:30 p.m. (Please enter through the back door, into the basement.)

The pastor would appreciate it if the ladies of the congregation would lend him their electric girdles for the pancake breakfast next Sunday morning.

The Ladies Bible Study will be held Thursday morning at 10. Lunch will be served in the Fellowship Hall after the ladies are done with the B.S.

22
TODAY'S QUOTE

"The secret of a good sermon is to have a good beginning and a good ending, then having the two as close together as possible."

George Burns

23
SEEN ON A BUMPER STICKER

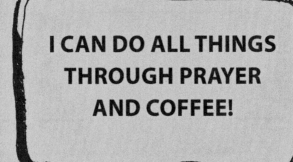

I CAN DO ALL THINGS THROUGH PRAYER AND COFFEE!

24
DID YOU KNOW?

Of all U.S. states, Alaska has the highest ratio
of unmarried men to unmarried women -
sparking the famous local saying, "The odds
are good, but the goods are odd."

25
TODAY'S QUOTE

"Being sinless must be easy for hermits.
They have no peer pressure."

Drew Cody

DID YOU KNOW?

"Cooties," those mysterious critters that have hampered many an elementary-school romance, are real.

Though more commonly known as "body lice," cooties are parasitic insects that can take up residence on humans and other warm-blooded creatures. Body lice are actually

something to be feared, as they can spread typhus fever. ("Cootie," incidentally, derives from the Malay word kutu, which means "biting insect.")

27
TODAY'S QUOTE

"Life was a lot simpler when what we honored was father and mother, rather than all major credit cards."

Robert Orben

THE NEW TESTAMENT
ACCORDING TO MRS. KLEFCORN'S GRADE SCHOOL SUNDAY SCHOOL CLASS

The New Testament appears in the Bible, right after the Old one. The New Testament is 2,000 years old, so why is it called "new?"

Jesus is the star of the New Testament. He was born in Bethlehem, in a barn. Also, Jesus was born on Christmas day, so you have to feel sorry for Him, having His birthday so close to Christmas and all. Jesus had 12 opossums. The worst one was Judas Asparagus. Judas was so evil that they named a terrible vegetable after him.

During His life, Jesus had many arguments with sinners like the Pharisees and the Republicans. Jesus was a great man. He healed many leopards. He even preached to some Germans on the Mount. But then the Republicans and other guys put Jesus on trial before Pontius, the Pilot. Pilot should have stuck up for Jesus, but he just washed his hands instead.

Jesus died for our sins, then came back to life again. He went up to Heaven. His return is foretold in the book of Revolution.

32
DID YOU KNOW?

Shortly after settling in Jamestown, the English colonists determined the proper dowry that a man was required to pay for a new bride. After careful deliberation, a sum was agreed upon: 120 pounds. Not pounds in British currency. One hundred and twenty pounds of tobacco.

33
A RIDDLE OVERHEARD AT A NATIONAL PASTORAL CONVENTION

Q: What do you need to make a small fortune in the ministry?

A: A large fortune.

34
TODAY'S QUOTE

"I just dropped my toothpaste.
I'm Crest-fallen."

Todd Hafer

35
BULLETIN BLOOPERS

The choir will be practicing every Wednesday evening – until they get it right.

A REMINDER: Prayer requests will be taken until we can take no more.

Fasting Group meets for breakfast Saturdays at Pancake Plaza.

We want your clothes for the Clothing Drive, and for Work Day, we want your body.

36
A HOLIDAY OBSERVATION

If your Christmas Eve service does not involve candles being held by some people who really shouldn't handle fire, you're missing one of the most exciting elements of the holy season.

37

An unwritten rule of Church League Basketball: Each squad must have a minimum of two
portly old guys – with corrective lenses –
and at least one knee brace per geezer.

TODAY'S QUOTE

"Many years ago, someone decided that a little friendly competition among churches would be healthy, fun, and spiritually enriching.

Shortly after that idea was dismissed, someone else came up with the concept of Church League Basketball."

H. J. Springston

A GRAVE MATTER

An elderly man decided it was time to visit his minister to discuss matters related to his funeral service.

"The first question that comes to mind," the minister said, "is whether you want to be buried or cremated . . ."

The old gentleman thought for a few moments, then replied, "I really don't have a preference. Surprise me!"

40
FUN THINGS TO SAY AT CHURCH POTLUCKS

"Is there a vegan meal available?"

"Is the angel food cake gluten-free?"

"Does the angel food cake contain any real angels?"

"What, exactly, are the rules about gluttony?"

"So, I guess 'drinking the Kool Aid' is OK now?"

"Is it cool for me to designate whom I'd like to be Heimliched by, just in case?"

41
🦱 TODAY'S QUOTE 🦱

"I have been drinking a lot of Smartwater lately. It's not working."

Todd Hafer

42
SOMETHING TO PONDER

When we were kids, why were the least comfortable, the itchiest, and least-flattering clothes we owned called our "church clothes?"

43
SIGN FROM GOD

HARRISVILLE CHURCH
We're looking for a few
good sinners!

WORDS OF GOLD?

A pastor's car broke down on his way home from Sunday service. He walked home, then called his town's only mechanic on Monday morning. The mechanic met the pastor where the stalled car sat and began his repairs.

"I'm going to go easy with you on the cost, Reverend," the mechanic said after several minutes.

"Thank you so much," the man of the cloth replied. "After all, I'm just a poor preacher."

"I know," the mechanic said. "I heard your sermon yesterday."

DID YOU KNOW?

To test the theory that a million monkeys with a million typewriters could produce a Shakespearean love sonnet, British researchers gave six short-tailed monkeys a computer, then sat back to observe the reaction. Some monkeys did hit a few keystrokes, mostly long strings of S's. But most of them used their computer as a toilet or beat it with rocks.

A PASTOR'S PROVERB

"Doubts are the ants in the pants of faith. They keep it awake and moving."

Rev. Frederick Buechner

47

SIGN FROM GOD

FORT COLLINS FELLOWSHIP CENTER
Visitors welcome.
Members expected.

48
TODAY'S QUOTE

"Sometimes I lie awake at night and I ask, 'Where have I gone wrong?' Then a voice says to me, 'This is going to take more than one night.'"

Charlie Brown

49
GREATER LOVE HATH NO GRANDMA THAN THIS . . .

At the age of 53, Geraldine Wesolowski actually gave birth to her own grandson. She was implanted with an egg from her daughter-in-law – that was fertilized by her son. She carried the baby to term as a literal labor of love.

50
A PREACHER'S PROVERB

"The length of a sermon should be directly related to the capacity of the average human bladder."

Rev. Jerry Springston

TOP 10 LEAST POPULAR BIBLICAL NAMES

10. Ananias

9. Sapphire

8. Pontius

7. Kevin

6. Methuselah

5. Jehoshaphat

4. Jezebel

3. Bathsheba

2. Mephibosheth

1. Judas

(Honorable Mention: Whore of Babylon, Herod, James the Lesser, Bildad the Shuhite, and Tricia.)

52

A church van is lot like a regular van, only it runs as much on prayer as it does on gasoline.

53
TODAY'S QUOTE

"Tonight I will dream of spruce.
But tomorrow I will dream of yew. Only yew."

Todd Hafer
(WHO NEVER GETS SYCAMORE TREE PUNS)

TOP FIVE CHURCH PICK-UP LINES

5. "Hey, baby, what's your spiritual gift?"

4. "No, this pew isn't saved, but I sure am!"

3. "This sermon is dull – wanna try
to start The Wave?"

2. "Do you know I can bench-press an entire
set of Bible commentaries?"

1. "Do you have a brother named Gabriel?
Because I am sure you're an angel!"

55
SEEN ON A BUMPER STICKER

DON'T LET THE CAR
FOOL YOU: MY TREASURES
ARE IN HEAVEN.

ONE DAY AT THE FIRST BAPTIST CHURCH OFFICE

Church Secretary Janet: "Pastor, there is a problem with your smartphone. There's moisture in the circuitry."

Pastor Bob: "Moisture in the circuitry? That doesn't make any sense. The air in this building is as dry as a desert."

Church Secretary Janet: "I'm telling you, sir, that there is moisture in the circuitry."

Pastor Bob: "That's ridiculous. Besides, you're not a techie. What do you know about circuitry? And where is my smartphone anyway?"

Church Secretary Janet: "At the bottom of the baptistery."

BULLETIN BLOOPERS

Eight new choir robes are currently needed, due to the addition of several new members and the deterioration of some older ones.

At tonight's evening service, the sermon topic will be "What Is Hell?" Come early and listen to our choir practice!

A bean supper will be held on Tuesday evening in the church hall. Music will follow.

Irving Benson and Jessie Carter were married on October 24 in our church. So ends a friendship that began in their school days.

This being Easter Sunday, we will ask Mrs. Lewis to come forward before the service and lay an egg on the altar.

58
TODAY'S QUOTE

"A good sermon should be like a woman's skirt – short enough to arouse interest but long enough to cover the essentials."

Ronald Knox

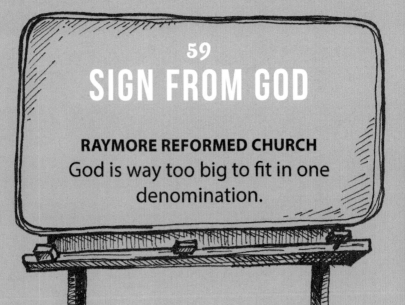

59
SIGN FROM GOD

RAYMORE REFORMED CHURCH
God is way too big to fit in one denomination.

60
SOMETHING TO PONDER

Why are church people so kind,
polite, and sweet-spirited – until you
try to sit in their pew?

61
DID YOU KNOW?

In captivity, orangutans have created a tool
out of a paper clip – and used it to pick the
locks on their cages!

KNOWING THE DRILL

An observation about those "Sword Drills" so many churches employ. Many children are surprised to find out, as they grow up and face life's challenges, that the ability to find verses in the Bible really-super-fast is not that helpful.

BULLETIN BLOOPERS

Do not miss Pastor Ted's moving massage tonight at 6 p.m.

The outreach committee needs 25 volunteers to call on people who are not afflicted with any church.

Worship Reminder: The congregation is asked to remain seated until the end of the recession.

64
TODAY'S QUOTE

"Don't say, 'Words cannot describe' something.
Try: We have many good words. Words matter.
They are the only thing that separate us from
the mimes."

Jedd Hafer

65
YOU KNOW YOU'RE A SPORTS FANATIC WHEN . . .

You refer to renewing your wedding
vows as a "contract extension."

66 TODAY'S QUOTE 99

"Behind every successful man stands a surprised mother-in-law."

Hubert Humphrey

TODAY'S TOP FIVE REASONS TO SMILE

There's always a chance that boring meeting
you have been dreading will get canceled.

That TV star who annoys you is about
to get his (or her!) show canceled.

Spring is never that far away.

That unpleasant task you're dreading?
You can probably delegate it.

You look a lot better than that
celebrity who just had another plastic surgery.

FREE TREES FOR THE PRESIDENT!

Being President of the United States comes with a lot of fringe benefits, one of which is a free Christmas tree. The National Christmas Tree Association has given a Christmas tree to every U.S. President and his family since Lyndon B. Johnson.

Incidentally, Franklin Pierce, the 14th President of the United States, was the first to put up a Christmas tree in the White House, but as he predated the National Christmas Tree Association, he had to procure his own tree. Still, Pierce started a tradition, albeit with one notable boycotter: Theodore Roosevelt, a staunch conservationist, refused to have a tree cut down, even to decorate the White House.

TODAY'S QUOTE

"Every reader who believes in telekinesis, please raise my hand!"

Jedd Hafer

TODAY'S TOP FIVE REASONS TO SMILE

Automated car washes – part labor-saving convenience, part amusement park ride.

They've finally created some energy bars that don't taste like cardboard.

Books are still one of the best bargains going.

Milk Duds are low-fat.

You're still pretty good at Ping-Pong.

71

Why is the most frightful, evil-looking person many children ever meet a leader at church camp?

TODAY'S QUOTE

"Vegetarian. That's an old Indian word meaning 'lousy hunter.'"

Andy Rooney

HAPPY HOLLY-DAYS

Holly, with its crimson berries and vivid green leaves, is one of the holiday season's most striking decorations. This plant has long been a part of various cultures' celebrations. In ancient times it was thought to be magical because of its unusually shiny leaves and ability to bear fruit in winter. Additionally, some religious poems and songs portray holly berries as a symbol of Christ and His death on the cross. However, holly is best enjoyed by the eyes, not the tongue. Holly berries, while tolerated by birds and wild animals, are mildly toxic to humans and can cause vomiting and diarrhea, two things that will not enhance one's holiday celebration.

BULLETIN BLOOPERS

Potluck supper Sunday at 5 p.m. Prayer and medication to follow.

Remember, on New Year's Eve the church will host an evening of fine dining, superb entertainment, and gracious hostility.

Attend our prayer breakfast next Saturday. You will hear an excellent speaker and heave a hearty meal!

Yet another Youth Group bonfire has been canceled. (We really might not plan any more Youth Group bonfires.)

A BEATITUDE, BY GEORGE

"Blessed is the man who, having nothing to say, abstains from giving wordy evidence of that fact."

George Eliot

SIGN FROM GOD

BUFFALO COMMUNITY CHURCH
Soul food served here!

TODAY'S TOP FIVE REASONS TO SMILE

Most elevators don't play
elevator music anymore.

Hello, national Do Not Call list;
goodbye, telemarketers.

Your signature looks cool; it would
make a great autograph.

Naps are in. (Call yours a "power nap"
if it makes you feel better.)

It takes 26 muscles to smile; just think of the
workout you'll get on your "happy days."

77
TODAY'S QUOTE

"Greater love hath no man than this; to attend
the Episcopal Church with his wife."

President Lyndon B. Johnson

79
REMINISCING

We grew up in a strict, fear-filled church.
The sign on the church lawn read:
BEWARE OF GOD.

Jedd and Todd Hafer

TODAY'S QUOTE

"Acting is not an important job in the scheme of things. Plumbing is."

Spencer Tracy

CHRISTMAS CRAZINESS

If Christmas seems like an especially crazy and frantic time of year – sheer bedlam, in fact – there is a good reason: The word "bedlam" is intrinsically linked to Christmas. In mid-thirteenth century London, there stood a monastery called St. Mary's of Bethlehem, in honor of the Biblical mother of Jesus. Later, the name of the monastery was shortened to Beth'lem, then later to simply Bedlam. At some point in the 1600s, Bedlam was turned from a monastery into a house of detention for the criminally insane.

THE PRODIGAL SON, IN THE KEY OF F

Feeling footloose and frisky, a frivolous, feather-brained fellow forced his fond, fawning father to fork over a fair share of the family farthings. Then, the flighty flibbertigibbet bade farewell and fled far to foreign fields, where he frittered his fabulous fortune, feasting famously among faithless fair-weather friends until, fleeced by his feckless, fun-loving fellows in folly, he found himself a feed-flinger in a festering, filthy farmyard.

Flummoxed, famished, filled with foreboding, and fairly facing famine, the frazzled fugitive found his faculties and returned to his father's farm. "Father, Father!" he forlornly fumbled, "I've flunked, flubbed, failed, and frivolously forfeited family favor. Phooey on me! Let me be as one of your flunkies. For even a fruitless flunkie would fare far, far better than I have fared. Fair enough?"

"Filial fidelity is fine," the father philosophized, "but, folks, the fugitive is found! Let fanfares flare! Let flags unfurl! Fetch the fatling, play that funky music, and let's have some fun!"

Unfortunately, older brother Frank was unforgiving. "Father!" he fumed

furiously. "Forsooth from this folly! Frankly, it's unfair. That fool forfeited his fortune!"

"Frank, Frank, Frank, Frank, Frank," the father confronted. "Don't fear nor fester. I'm your fan. Your coffers are fairly filled to overflowing with farthings. But your phantom brother is finally and fortuitously back in the fold. For many fortnights, I've fantasized about this fabulous and festive feast. So focus on fun, not funds – or flake off."

So, a fatheaded, foolish fugitive found fulfillment.

Furthermore, the father's fond forgiveness formed the foundation for the former fugitive's future welfare. For a faithful father loves forever.

(We're Finally Finished!)

Todd and Jedd Hafer

TODAY'S QUOTE

"Trying to craft the perfect metaphor is a bitter lizard."

Todd Hafer

DID YOU KNOW?

Among baseball's 1987 year-ending best-of awards, this oddity appears. A minor-league second-string catcher named Dave Bresnahan is named (with tongue in cheek) Sports Person of the Year by the Chicago Tribune. The feat that earned Bresnahan the award? He peeled and sculpted a potato to look like a baseball, which he then threw wildly into left field during a game, luring an opposing runner on third base to try to score. When that runner reached home plate, Bresnahan used the real baseball to tag him out. (The following year, Bresnahan's team, the Williamsport Bills, re-tired his number.)

REMINISCING

We used to ask our mom repeatedly, "Do you think we'll be famous authors when we grow up?" She would reply, "If it's God's will." We'd counter, "But how will we know if it's God's

will? Will He give us a sign? And when will we know? Mom would just shake her head and say, "You know, for a couple of janitors, you ask a lot of questions."

Jedd and Todd Hafer

TODAY'S QUOTE

"I used to date an Amish girl.
She drove me buggy."

Jedd Hafer

DID YOU KNOW?

In 1943, a friend gave coach John Wooden a small wooden cross, which he carried in his pocket from that moment on. "I held it in my hand during games, during times of tension. It reminded me who is in control," Wooden explained. "It probably is a good thing for officials that I had that cross in my hand when a bad call was made."

88

SIGN FROM GOD

UNITED CHURCH OF CHRIST
Under the same management
for 2,000-plus years!

90
REMINISCING

People in our church believed in giving till it hurts. Unfortunately for our dad, the pastor, they had a very low pain threshold.

Jedd and Todd Hafer

91
TODAY'S QUOTE

"Here's a piece of advice: Don't hang out with algebra teachers. They have too many problems."

Drew Cody

92
A PASTORAL PROVERB

"Receiving accolades from your congregation after a powerful sermon is like smoking a cigar; it won't hurt you if you don't inhale."

Rev. Robert St. John

93
TODAY'S QUOTE

"I don't want to say my congregation is musically unsophisticated, but about half of them think a cantata is an entrée at Taco Bell."

Rev. Jerry Springston

94
TODAY'S QUOTE

"Here's something to do for fun. Go into a bakery and tell the baker you want a pie, cut into 3.14 slices."

George House

95
SEEN ON THE DOOR OF A CHURCH NURSERY

"We will not all sleep, but we will all be changed . . ."

1 Corinthians 15:51

REMINISCING

One of our elementary school teachers thought we were too obsessive. So she made us write, "I will not obsess!" 1,000 times on the blackboard.

Jedd and Todd Hafer

TODAY'S QUOTE

"The man who can always walk with his head above the crowd . . . is probably 8 feet tall."

Drew Cody

FRUITS AND VEGGIES:

NOT ALWAYS GOOD FOR YOU

During Game 7 of the 1934 World Series, Joe "Ducky" Medwick of the St. Louis Cardinals smacked a 6th-inning triple and knocked over Detroit Tiger third baseman Marv Owens on his way to the bag. The two men exchanged shoves and harsh words.

When Medwick returned to his post in left field for the bottom of the inning, Tiger fans showed their displeasure by pelting him with whatever projectiles they could find, including an assortment of fruits and vegetables. Ducky could not duck them all, and he was forced to leave the game for his own safety - a World Series first.

(The Cards won the game 11-zip.)

99
IN THE SERVICE

A pastor and his young daughter stood at a World War II Memorial. The pastor explained to the girl, "Honey, this is a monument to brave people who died in the service."

"That's so sad," the daughter replied. "Was it in the 8:30 or 11 o'clock service?"

100
REMINISCING

In high school, we hated history. The teacher kept repeating himself.

Jedd and Todd Hafer

101
TODAY'S QUOTE

"A Mennonite by any other name is
an Anabaptist."

Todd Hafer

102
WALL 1,
QUARTERBACK 0

During the first half of a 1997 game against
the New York Giants, Washington Redskin
quarterback Gus Frerotte scampered into the
end zone for a touchdown. The QB first celebrated by spiking the football into the stadium
wall. Then, apparently not satisfied, Frerotte
head-butted the wall, which was padded (albeit padded concrete). He sprained his neck in
the process and was unable to start the
second half of the game.

TODAY'S QUOTE

"When I was a kid, I used to imagine animals running under my bed. I told my dad, and he solved the problem quickly. He cut the legs off the bed."

Lou Brock

YOU KNOW YOU'RE A SPORTS FANATIC WHEN . . .

You've submitted church prayer request cards for a "groin pull."

105

Talk about midlife crises: We know a guy named Steve who decided to become a monk at age 50. He left his wife, Ruth, and walked away, ruthlessly.

TODAY'S QUOTE

"Why do birds suddenly appear every time you are near? Is it because you smell like stale bread crumbs?"

Jedd Hafer

107

ASK THE THEOLOGICAL KNOW-HOW DUDES

QUESTION: Our children really want to trick-or-treat this Halloween, but our church frowns on this holiday. What should we do?

ANSWER: Boy, that's a tough question. Hmmm. Perhaps a compromise between kids

and church would be in order. You could do what our parents always did. We didn't actually get to trick-or-treat. Instead, every year Mom and Dad dressed us up as raccoons and told us to rummage through the neighborhood garbage for our "treats."

Jedd and Todd Hafer

TODAY'S QUOTE

"I am so glad I went to college in the pre-Internet era. I can proudly say that every co-ed who pretended to like me was a real person."

Todd Hafer

ASK THE THEOLOGICAL KNOW-HOW DUDES

QUESTION: I've been to several Christian stores, but I can't find any decent manna. What gives?

ANSWER: Don't be dismayed. A good manna is hard to find.

Jedd and Todd Hafer

TODAY'S QUOTE

"Is it OK if I fake my admiration for your false eyelashes, acrylic nails, and fake breasts?"

Jedd Hafer

REMINISCING

You want to know how uptight our childhood church was? The gates were made of over-wrought iron.

Jedd and Todd Hafer

ASK THE THEOLOGICAL KNOW-HOW DUDES

QUESTION: When is Easter this year?

ANSWER: It is on Easter Sunday.

QUESTION: OK, but when is
National Redundancy Day?

ANSWER: It will be celebrated on Tuesday,
August 22nd, and again on Wednesday, August 23rd. For more information on this holiday, contact The Department of Redundancy
Department, New York, New York. 10101-0101.

Jedd and Todd Hafer

112
TODAY'S QUOTE

"Some people go to church and think about fishing; I go fishing and think about God."

Taylor Morgan

116
TODAY'S QUOTE

"Give me ambiguity . . . or give me something else. Whatever."

Drew Cody

ASK THE THEOLOGICAL KNOW-HOW DUDES

QUESTION: How do you feel about women in the ministry?

ANSWER: What kind of incendiary question is that? Are you trying to get your lovable Theological Know-How Dudes in trouble? Let's just leave it at this. We think women are intelligent, capable, and mature people who can succeed wherever God leads them. Consider the National Basketball Association, which recently hired its first-ever women referees. These officials have done an incredible job. There's been only one noticeable difference between the women and their male counterparts. When a female ref calls a foul on a player, she also brings up all the fouls the player committed in the past three months.

Jedd and Todd Hafer

118

Church softball. For women it's a chance to release some long pent-up aggression. For men,
it's a chance to compete on a large grassy area
that someone else has to mow.

TODAY'S QUOTE

"Beware the self-made man; he tends to worship his creator."

Drew Cody

SIGN FROM GOD

EASTSIDE COMMUNITY CHURCH
Psalm Reader on Duty

121
SEEN ON A BUMPER STICKER

HWJD
(How Would Jesus Drive?)

124
TODAY'S QUOTE

"I have been trying to learn our church's new computer system. This is what I have learned: Artificial intelligence is no match for 100-percent natural stupidity."

Rev. Jerry Springston

BULLETIN BLOOPERS

Barbara remains in the hospital and needs blood donors for more transfusions. She is also having trouble sleeping and requests CDs of Pastor Jack's sermons.

The rector will preach his farewell message tonight, after which the choir will sing, "Break Forth Into Joy!"

Next Thursday there will be tryouts for the choir. They need all the help they can get.

Remember the big all-church swap meet next Saturday in City Park. Husbands, bring your wives and get a great bargain!

123
SEEN ON A BUMPER STICKER
(OF A HEARSE)

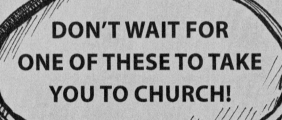

DON'T WAIT FOR ONE OF THESE TO TAKE YOU TO CHURCH!

126
REMINISCING

Our church camp's most distinguishing characteristic was its mosquitoes. When one of these bat-sized bloodsuckers bit you, he'd take so much blood that he'd give you a glass of orange juice and a sugar cookie afterwards.

Jedd and Todd Hafer

ASK THE THEOLOGICAL KNOW-HOW DUDES

QUESTION: We're having our first child – a boy – next month. We'd like to give him a Biblical name. We're thinking Matthew. Do you approve?

ANSWER: No, we're sorry. Matthew is a fine Biblical name, but it's too common. These days, every Tom, Dick, and Harry is named Matthew.

Jedd and Todd Hafer

CHRISTMAS SHOPPING 101

Who can say he or she truly looks forward to the madness that is Christmas shopping? In an effort to avoid the crowds and long lines, many people have resorted to online shopping or homemade gifts. Both are better options than the one sought by a man who found himself in front of a judge one holiday season.

"Do you understand the charges brought against you?" the judge asked.

"Yes," the man answered. "I have been charged with doing my Christmas shopping early."

Puzzled, the judge queried, "Just how early were you doing your Christmas shopping anyway?"

The man shrugged. "Before the stores opened."

128
YOU KNOW YOU'RE A SPORTS FANATIC WHEN . . .

You've started a love poem to your sweetie with the words, "Two, four, six, eight, who do I appreciate?"

"JINGLE BELLS":
THE UNTOLD STORY

Although it's a Christmas favorite, this dashing song was originally written for another holiday. Circa 1857, James Lord Pierpont, an organist for a church in Savannah, Georgia, wrote the song for his Sunday school class's Thanksgiving celebration. "Jingle Bells" was so well-received that Pierpont revived it for the church's Christmas festivities.

Incidentally, this song has historical significance, as it is the first carol to be broadcast from outer space. On December 16, 1965, the Gemini 6 astronauts played the song on bells and a harmonica that they had snuck onboard their spacecraft.

130
TODAY'S QUOTE

"Either I do not understand today's fashions, or there is a rodeo clown convention in town."

Jedd Hafer

136
YOU'VE BEEN WARNED

If you're at a congregational business meeting, and someone says, "To make a long story short . . ." it's already too late.

CHRISTMAS IS . . . WHITE (MAYBE)

Lots of people dream of a white Christmas, but unless you live in Alaska, chances are that those dreams might not be realized. Based on averages over the past 30 years, the National Climatic Data Center lists only five contiguous U.S. cities that stand a 100 percent chance of boasting at least an inch of snow on Christmas Day. They are:

Marquette, MI

Sault Ste. Marie, MI

Hibbing, MN

International Falls, MN

Stampede Pass, WA

What are your city's chances of a white Christmas? Check the NCDC's map of Christmas snow likelihood at <u>www.ncdc.noaa.gov/oa/climate</u>

TODAY'S QUOTE

"One time I went to a museum where all the work had been done by children. The museum had all the paintings up on refrigerators."

Steven Wright

TODAY'S QUOTE

"For marriage to be a success, every woman and every man should have her or his own bathroom. The end."

Catherine Zeta-Jones

134
YOU KNOW YOU'RE A SPORTS FANATIC WHEN . . .

The air freshener in your car bears the scent of "New Catcher's Mitt."

135
SOMETHING TO PONDER

What if God is asking US for a sign?

TODAY'S QUOTE

"Put your hand on a hot stove for a minute and it seems like an hour; sit next to a pretty woman for an hour and it seems like a minute. That's relativity."

Albert Einstein

DID YOU KNOW?

At age 92, actor George Burns played a younger character in the movie "18 Again." In the movie, Burns' character is only 81. To help support the movie, Burns also recorded a hit single by the same name.

139
TODAY'S QUOTE

"My husband wanted one of those big-screen TVs for his birthday. So I just moved his chair closer to the TV we already have."

Wendy Liebman

140
DID YOU KNOW?

On November 9, 1813 Andrew Jackson led 2,000 troops into eastern Alabama to expel Creek Indians from the area. According to legend, a Creek medicine man placed a curse on the area as he was marched away. That land is now occupied by auto racing's Talladega Superspeedway.

141
TODAY'S QUOTE

"I want my husband to take me in his arms and whisper those three little words that all women long to hear: 'You were right.'"

Kelly Smith

142
SPEAKING OF SPORTS . . .

"I know I am getting better at golf because I am hitting fewer spectators."

President Gerald Ford

143
YOU'VE BEEN WARNED

If you prove to be a talented church volunteer, you'll be "volunteered" for everything. But if you are really, really talented, you'll be able to get out of it.

144
SOMETHING TO PONDER

Can God inspire a sermon so boring that even God cannot stay awake through it?

A PASTOR'S PLEA

"Please live a good life. I don't want to lie at your funeral."

Rev. Robert St. John

DID YOU KNOW?

Finland's Tommi Huotari needed a new challenge after becoming one of the world's best potato throwers. So the Finnish hurler moved on . . . to tossing cellphones. At age 38, he won the World Cellphone Throwing Championship. His winning effort was 294 feet, almost the length of a football field.

147
TAKING 1,594 FOR THE TEAM

On his 12th birthday, David Witthoft gained national publicity, just for changing his shirt. The shirt in question was his beloved Brett Favre jersey – which David wore faithfully for more than four years (1,594 consecutive days, to be precise). The shirt was a Christmas present the boy received when he was seven.

148
TODAY'S QUOTE

"I wish I never would have bought that set of cow bookends. Every morning, I awake to find them tipped over."

Todd Hafer

FAIR TRADE?

Amid the post-season wheelings and dealings
of the 1987 Major League Baseball season,
relief pitcher Dickie Noles stood out
from the crowd. During the
season, the Chicago Cubs traded the right-
hander to Detroit, for a player to be named
later. In post-season talks between the two
teams, it was agreed that Noles himself would
be that "player to be named later." Thus, Noles
became the first player in MLB history to
be traded for himself!

150
TODAY'S QUOTE

"If you want to know what God thinks of money, just look at the people he gave it to."

Dorothy Parker

151
TODAY'S QUOTE

"Do you ever feel like a hammock in a land where all the trees are too far apart?"

Jedd Hafer

A VOICE FROM ABOVE

Two retired outdoorsmen from Texas traveled to Minnesota for some ice fishing. After setting up their tent and sorting their equipment, they began to drill a hole in the ice. As they fired up their chainsaw, they heard a booming voice from above them: "There are no fish under that ice!"

Startled, the men gawked at each other, wide-eyed. One of them tilted his head to the sky. "Is . . . is that you, Lord?" he asked.

The voice boomed again: "No, I'm the owner of this ice-skating rink, and I'm telling you two for the last time – there are no fish under that ice!"

153

When a pastor says, "I have a little project for you," his children know that he means, "I need you to shovel mountains of snow from the church parking lot – armed with one snow shovel, one army shovel, and one broken plastic dustpan."

154
LOST IN TATTOO TRANSLATION

NBA player Marquis Daniels got a Chinese tattoo that he believed to represent his initials. The tat's actual translation? "Big woman standing on a roof."

155
LOST IN TATTOO TRANSLATION, PART 2

NBA veteran Shawn Marion thought his Chinese tattoo meant "Matrix," which is his nickname. The tat's true meaning? "Demon Bird Moth Balls."

ASK THE THEOLOGICAL KNOW-HOW DUDES

QUESTION: I'm contemplating attending Bible college. What do you think I should do?

ANSWER: You asked the right guys. We heartily encourage you to attend the Bible college or university of your choice - especially if that choice is Biola University (because our Uncle Ron works there). You'll lay a firm foundation for your future. You'll be encouraged by the other young Christians preparing for a lifetime of service to the Lord. You'll grow in Christian knowledge. You'll meet godly friends. And, when it's all through, you'll have a really cool tassel to hang from your rear-view mirror! One more suggestion: Major in communications, as we did. That way, after you graduate and are able to score a job bagging groceries, you'll be able to say, "Paper or plastic?" and really get your message across.

Jedd and Todd Hafer

YOU KNOW IT'S TIME TO GET BACK IN SHAPE WHEN . . .

You try to straighten out the
wrinkles in your socks, and then
realize you aren't wearing socks.

Even when you stay home,
your back goes out.

Getting ready for a night
on the town, it takes you twice
as long to look half as good.

Most of the names of your Facebook
friends start with "Dr."

It takes you longer to rest up
than it did to get tired.

158
TODAY'S QUOTE

"I cannot do tai chi without
spilling my chai tea."

Todd Hafer

159
SPEAKING OF SPORTS . . .

"Little boys, when they are growing up, dream
of doing two things – playing Major League
Baseball and joining the circus. I played for the
New York Yankees and got to do both."

Greg Nettles

160
TODAY'S QUOTE

"**LIFE LESSON:** Cough syrup is great for coughs. Not so great on pancakes."

Todd Hafer

161
YOU KNOW YOU'RE A SPORTS FANATIC WHEN . . .

You insist on having your ankles taped before you mow the lawn.

162
TODAY'S QUOTE

"This too shall pass. Now
would be good."

Dee Ann Stewart

163
SEEN ON A BUMPER STICKER

COINCIDENCE:
When God chooses to
remain anonymous.

164
SPEAKING OF SPORTS . . .

"The English are not very spiritual people, so they invented cricket to give them some idea of eternity."

George Bernard Shaw

168
TODAY'S QUOTE

"Don't spend money on those chewable candy–vitamins. All vitamins are chewable. You just have to want it!"

Todd Hafer

165

You know your church potluck dinner is sketchy when the youth group's pet goat would rather eat the shingles on the church roof rather than consume anything in the Fellowship Hall.

169
YOU KNOW YOU'RE A SPORTS FANATIC WHEN . . .

Reading box scores is part of
your morning devotions.

170
TODAY'S QUOTE

"A fishing rod is a stick with a hook at one end
and a fool at the other."

Samuel Johnson

ASK THE THEOLOGICAL KNOW-HOW DUDES

QUESTION: I am a 12-year-old boy. Therefore I belch. The problem is that we recently had Pastor Tompkins over for dinner, and I belched in front of him. Now I'm grounded for a month. I've heard in some cultures it's actually polite to belch. Can you research this and get me un-grounded?

ANSWER: Sorry, our little 12-year-old burping buddy. It's simply poor manners to belch in front of Pastor Tompkins. Next time, let him belch first.

Jedd and Todd Hafer

TODAY'S QUOTE

"Love teaches even asses to dance."

French proverb

YOU KNOW YOU'RE A SPORTS FANATIC WHEN . . .

Your family reunions are sponsored by Under Armour.

TODAY'S QUOTE

"Is a frittata just a quiche that didn't
want it bad enough?"

Todd Hafer

175

The Hafer brothers hate skiing
because it combines three of our least–
favorite things: falling down, pain, and cold.

YOU KNOW YOU'RE A SPORTS FANATIC WHEN . . .

You think that prison is better than marriage, because in prison they let you play softball on weekends.

TODAY'S QUOTE

"I recently read a list of the top 10 puns. How many puns made me laugh? No pun in ten did."

Jedd Hafer

178
YOU KNOW YOU'RE A SPORTS FANATIC WHEN . . .

You keep trying to "friend"
Ted Williams's frozen head
on Facebook.

179
TODAY'S QUOTE

"I am unfollowing the Yeti on
Twitter. I am tired of reading,
'Raaargh!' thirteen times a day."

Todd Hafer

TODAY'S QUOTE

"The good Lord didn't create anything without a purpose, but the fly comes close."

Mark Twain

SIGN FROM GOD

CHRISTIAN FELLOWSHIP CHURCH
Church Parking Only!
Trespassers will be baptized.

182
YOU KNOW YOU'RE A SPORTS FANATIC WHEN . . .

You have sung your school's fight song to one of your children as a lullaby.

183
TODAY'S QUOTE

"To be clever enough to get all of the money, one must be stupid enough to want it."

G.K. Chesterton

184
CHURCH BULLETIN BLOOPERS, SPORTS EDITION

Men's Basketball this Tuesday. Watch as we give Our Lady of Sorrows something to cry about.

No dunking on the basketball court at St. Theresa's. (If you can think of a way to sprinkle, go for it.)

Softball game against Our Lady of Prophecy next Thursday cancelled due to rain.

Trust us.

TODAY'S QUOTE

"Love is the thing that enables a woman to sing while she mops up the floor after her husband has walked across it in his barn boots."

Anonymous Hoosier farmer

DID YOU KNOW?

The Denver, Colorado police department has begun to reward courteous, law-abiding citizens with free pizza. Officers hand out Papa John's gift cards that read, "You caught me doing something right."

187
YOU KNOW YOU'RE A SPORTS FANATIC WHEN . . .

Your annual Christmas letter
contains the phrase "strained glute."

188
TODAY'S QUOTE

"In love, as in other matters, the
young are just beginners."

Isaac Bashevis Singer

ON FOOTBALL AND FANTASY . . .

Self-proclaimed "fantasy-football widow" Allison Lodish (whose husband belongs to 10 fantasy football leagues) gained national publicity after forming WAFS – Women Against Fantasy Sports. The organization's website features a message board for members to post their laments – and also sells merchandise, such as undergarments with mottoes like CLOSED FOR THE FANTASY SEASON.

192
DID YOU KNOW?

Sharpshooter Annie Oakley nailed 98 of 100 clay pigeons in an exhibition at a North Carolina gun club – at the age of 61!

193
ROUGH & READY TEDDY

Politicians aren't usually thought of as rough-and-tumble guys. But President Teddy Roosevelt's outdoorsman lifestyle made him one tough customer. How tough? While campaigning for a return to the White House in 1912, he was shot in a dispute with a saloon keeper. With the bullet still lodged in his chest, Roosevelt delivered his campaign speech, as scheduled.

TODAY'S QUOTE

"Thought for the Day: Simon Peter and Andrew were fishermen; what did they do for vacation – take a week off to go accounting?"

Dan Taylor

SEEN ON A BUMPER STICKER

THOSE WHO CAN, DO. THOSE WHO CANNOT, START GIVING SEMINARS ON IT.

THE TRUTH ABOUT OTTO THE ORANGE

In honor of upstate New York's heritage, which includes salt production and serving as home to the Onondaga and Oneida Indian tribes, Syracuse University named its athletic teams the Saltine Warriors – nicknamed the Orange-men. Today, thanks to political correctness, those same teams are known simply as the Orange. The school's current mascot is Otto the Orange, a character with hands where ears would normally be located. Moreover, Otto does not seem to represent a true orange. The school's website describes him as merely a "fuzzy and fruity figure."

DID YOU KNOW?

The dedication ceremony for the Abraham Lincoln Memorial, honoring the "Great Emancipator," was segregated.

TODAY'S QUOTE

"I am trying to think of a really good cliché, but I keep drawing a blank!"

Todd Hafer

199

YOU KNOW YOU'RE A SPORTS FANATIC WHEN . . .

You refer to loosening your pants during a big meal as "the seventh-inning stretch."

200

THANK YOU FOR CALLING OUR COMPANY . . .

". . . your phone call is very important to us. Just not important enough for us to allow you to talk to an actual human being any time in the near future. Meanwhile, please enjoy 23 minutes of on-hold music, as you rock out with Yanni! While you wait, and wait . . . and wait, please remember how important you are to us."

TODAY'S QUOTE

"I want to start a ministry for disgruntled former employees. I would like to help them become gruntled once again."

Jedd Hafer

YOU KNOW YOU'RE A SPORTS FANATIC WHEN . . .

Your riding lawn mower has a number and sponsor logos on it.

THE FIVE BEST WAYS TO KILL AN INNOVATIVE IDEA

"Have we tried that before?
Has anyone tried that before?"

"That sounds expensive."

"Who's going to take on the extra work?"

"Why change? Things are OK the way they are."

"Let's form a committee to explore
this idea further!"

204

Many theologians are unaware that the prophet John was "John the Episcopalian," "John the Presbyterian," "John the Congregationalist," and "John the Reformed Lutheran" before finally settling on being "The Baptist" – much to the delight of his wife, Anna Baptist.

YESTERDAY
(A TECHNOLOGY SONG)

Yesterday,

All those backups seemed a waste of pay.

Now my database has flown away.

Oh, I believe in yesterday.

Suddenly,

There's not half the files there used to be.

There's a millstone hanging

on to me.

My system crashed so suddenly!

I clicked something wrong,

What it was I could not say.

Now my data's gone, and I long for yesterday-

ay-ay-ay!

ASK THE THEOLOGICAL KNOW-HOW DUDES

QUESTION: I'm confused about the "end times." Where do you guys stand? Are you premillennialists? Postmillennialists? Amillennialists?

ANSWER: We are panmillennialists. We firmly believe that everything will pan out in the end.

Jedd and Todd Hafer

A KNOCKOUT OF A BIG LEAGUE DEBUT

It's said that it's not how you start; it's how you finish. Baseball's Billy Herman is living proof. In his first big-league at-bat, Herman faced fireballing Cincinnati Reds' pitcher Si Johnson. Herman fouled a Johnson pitch into the dirt behind home plate, and the ball ricocheted upward, nailing Herman in the back of the head.

The 22-year-old second baseman was knocked cold. He was carried off the field on a stretcher. Some athletes might have considered a career change after such an embarrassing and painful beginning. But Herman recovered quickly–both physically and psychologically. He was soon back on the field. He played for 16 years in the Major Leagues, leading the National League in put-outs seven times, collecting 2,345 hits, and posting a career batting average of .304. All this, despite leaving baseball for two years to fight in World War II. He was elected to the Baseball Hall of Fame in 1975.

Today, more than six decades after Herman retired, two of his records are still on the books. He holds the National League mark for most put-outs by a second baseman. And no one in MLB history has topped his record of five opening-day hits, set way back in 1936.

TODAY'S QUOTE

"I have decided to live each day as if it is my last. So if you need me, I will be sitting in my rocking chair, wrapped in a blanket, staring out the window, and coughing weakly."

Todd Hafer

WEDDING PROJECTILES FROM AROUND THE WORLD

American weddings feature the tossing of rice or birdseed, but here are the projectiles of choice for weddings in other parts of the world:

Turkey: candy

North Africa: figs and dates

France: wheat

Italy: coins, candy, and dried fruit

Greece: candied almonds

Former Czech Republic: dried peas

Mexico: red beads

Korea: nuts and dates

India: flower petals and puffed rice

210
SPEAKING OF SPORTS . . .

"I fought Sugar Ray Robinson so many
times, I'm surprised I'm not diabetic."

Jake LaMotta

211
DID YOU KNOW?

In an arranged marriage, five-year-old Sir
Temulji Nariman married the newly dubbed
Lady Nariman, who was also only five. Despite
the odd beginning, the couple stayed married
for 88 years, until Sir Temulji's death, at the
age of 93.

TODAY'S QUOTE

"I plan to stop eating cold turkey forever, starting right now! If only there were an idiom to describe my bold decision . . ."

Jedd Hafer

DID YOU KNOW?

Wedding cake was originally designed to be thrown at the bride and groom, just as we toss rice or birdseed today. Fortunately, the projectile version of wedding cake was not frosted, making the custom less messy for both the hurlers and their targets.

AIN'T THAT A KICK?

Cardinals rookie placekicker Bill Gramatica was excited after booting a 42-yard first-quarter field goal in a game against the New York Giants. So excited that he leaped into the air to celebrate. Unfortunately, he landed awkwardly and tore his anterior cruciate ligament and cartilage in his knee. He missed the rest of the season.

TODAY'S QUOTE

"Is anyone else in our country embarrassed that the drug dealers have embraced the metric system more readily than the rest of us?"

Todd Hafer

216
GOOD KNIGHT!

Prior to the 1984 Summer Olympics, Coach Bobby Knight cut the following players from the United States basketball team: Charles Barkley, Karl Malone, John Stockton, Joe Dumars, and Terry Porter. (Players who made the team include Jeff Turner, Joe Kleine, Steve Alford, and Jon Koncak. And, oh yeah, a shooting guard named Michael Jordan.)

DID YOU KNOW?

When the Beatles recorded their
hit song "Love Me Do," John Lennon was still
a struggling young musician. He played the
instrumental part of the song on a harmonica
he shoplifted before the recording session.

TODAY'S QUOTE

"I'm an ex-Drifter. I was never part of the
vocal group, but I used to do a lot of
aimless wandering."

Jedd Hafer

219

It is time to face facts: Sometimes, the "special
music" in church is not all that special.
Especially when it involves the tuba.

220
DID YOU KNOW?

Before a "hot date," women of ancient Rome attempted to make their skin soft and sweet-smelling by bathing in tubs filled with donkey milk, mixed with a bit of swan's fat.

221
SPEAKING OF SPORTS . . .

"Stay alert – you can observe
a lot by watching."

Yogi Berra

DID YOU KNOW?

If you have ever stolen a kiss under the mistletoe, you should thank the ancient Druids. The Druids believed the mistletoe plant to be a symbol of peace, so the politically tenuous negotiations between warring Celtic tribes were held under branches sporting mistletoe plants. Under the mistletoe, the negotiators would lay down their arms as a sign of truce. Later, when the Celts converted to Christianity, mistletoe survived as an emblem of goodwill and friendship.

Eventually, mistletoe began to be hung over doorways at Christmastime, and guests were often greeted at these doorways with a friendly kiss.

The custom continued to morph, and during the 18th century in England, it became permissible for an unmarried man to kiss any unmarried woman whom he happened to catch beneath the famous parasitic plant.

Ironically, while mistletoe can be enjoyable to kiss under, it should not be eaten. Both its leaves and berries are toxic and potentially lethal, to humans and pets.

223
A TREE BY ANY OTHER NAME

Stanford University's athletic teams were once the Indians. In a nod to cultural sensitivity, the moniker was switched to the Cardinal. However, the school's mascot is neither an Indian nor a bird. (Nor an official in the Catholic Church.) It's a dancing, prank-pulling tree, known, cleverly as "the Tree," – which is one of the most-ridiculed mascots in all of college athletics.

224
TODAY'S QUOTE

"What do you do when you come
to a spork in the road?"

Todd Hafer

225
SPEAKING OF SPORTS . . .

"The secret of managing is to keep the guys
who hate you away from the guys who are still
making up their minds."

Casey Stengel

LEGENDARY BASEBALL MANAGER

DID YOU KNOW?

April of 1963 will forever be known as a prophetic month for Major League Baseball pitcher Gaylord Perry. After consistently struggling at the plate that spring, Perry told the media, "They'll put a man on the moon before I hit a home run." More than six years later, on July 20, 1969, Perry hit his first (and only) big-league dinger – just hours after Neil Armstrong stepped onto the moon's surface.

TODAY'S QUOTE

"Hot dogs are just offal!"

Jedd Hafer

SPECIAL MUSIC
WHAT TO DO WHEN IT'S NOT SO SPECIAL

Music has never been a strong point at Broomfield Baptist Church, our childhood church home. Thus, one of the greatest tests of our self-control during worship services was the "special music." Or the "ministry in music," the "witness in song," or "a husband and wife with a guitar and too much free time."

At most churches, a talented individual from the congregation will select an appropriate Third Day or Steven Curtis Chapman back-up track, add a few tasteful dance moves, and deliver a pleasant-sounding, spiritually uplifting performance.

At BBC, a farmer named Clem would sing "Do Lord," accompanying himself with the musical spoons. Or, our favorite member of the music militia, Mrs. Smithstein, would waddle to the stage, toting a tuba the size of a Sherman tank.

Mrs. Smithstein typically graced us with two or twelve old-time gospel favorites. Frightened children would scatter, as Mrs. S's face grew redder and redder. Adults found it hard not to burst out laughing. Mrs. S found it hard not to burst–period.

When Mrs. S and her tuba were finished assaulting some perfectly innocent songs, our dad would come to her side and say something like, "Thank you, Mrs. Smithstein. Those . . . uh, songs were uniquely and sincerely rendered." That's because he could not say,

"Your tuba playing sounds like a herd of flatulent wildebeests."

Dad's responses to Mrs. Smithstein are perfect–subtly honest and inoffensive. This is important because it would be wrong to be too blunt. That would have hurt Mrs. Smithstein. And she has a right hook that can take down a bison.

So, if you ever find yourself in the awkward position of trying to compliment someone in your church after he or she has butchered your favorite song, follow Reverend Hafer's lead. For example:

"I gotta tell you, Wendell, when Martin Luther wrote 'A Mighty Fortress' hundreds of years ago, I bet he never envisioned that one day you'd play his masterpiece on a homemade wax-paper-and-comb kazoo!"

Or, "Wow, Mrs. Gackout! How many people in the whole world can yodel 'Bringing in the Sheaves' while accompanying themselves on the accordion? Dressing as Heidi was a nice touch as well."

We Hafers aren't known for our extraordinary tact and diplomacy, but we have learned not to discourage people from sharing their gifts. So, give the above technique a try. It's important to make your local minstrels feel special, because they are. Even when their music isn't.

230
DID YOU KNOW?

Stay-at-home dad Michael Thompson's wife was content to let her husband mind the kids while she worked. However, Thompson ended up making a huge financial contribution to the family one memorable year. He won $1 million in a fantasy-fishing contest.

231
SPEAKING OF SPORTS . . .

"I haven't been able to slam-dunk the basketball for the past five years. Or, for the thirty-eight years before that, either."

Dave Barry

TODAY'S QUOTE

"I believe I have discovered a direct correlation between the complexity of a person's Star-bucks drink order and how big of a jerk he is."

Todd Hafer

SOMETHING TO PONDER

Did they serve iceberg lettuce on the Titanic?

234

You know your pastor has delivered an effective "altar call" when even a stray pet from the neighborhood comes forward!

235

YOU KNOW YOU'RE A SPORTS FANATIC WHEN . . .

Your marriage therapist asks you to name your "favorite position," and you respond, "Shortstop."

236

A FISHY TRADE

During the 1998 minor-league baseball season, the Independent League's Pacific Suns traded pitcher Ken Krahenbuhl to the Greenville (MS) Bluesmen for a player to be named later, an undisclosed sum of cash, and 10 pounds of Mississippi catfish.

TODAY'S QUOTE

"Freelance writing is my get-rich-slowly scheme. And, dude, it's working!"

Todd Hafer

DID YOU KNOW?

Legendary Oregon track coach Bill Bowerman invented the modern running shoe tread by molding a rubber sole using his wife's waffle iron. Bowerman founded a shoe company called Blue Ribbon Sports to sell his waffle-soled shoes. Several years later, the company adopted its new name, Nike.

239
A FISHY EXCUSE

Saint Peter halted a man at the entrance to heaven. "I'm sorry," the saint said, "but I cannot admit you. You've told too many lies."

"C'mon, Pete, give me a break," the man pleaded. "After all, you were once a fisherman yourself!"

240
YOU KNOW YOU'RE A SPORTS FANATIC WHEN . . .

You refer to dying as "joining the Senior Tour."

TODAY'S QUOTE

"Here's a marriage tip: Don't diet together. Two people should never be that cranky simultaneously."

Drew Cody

DID YOU KNOW?

During the 1970 Apollo 13 mission, astronauts used duct tape to fashion two CO_2 filters that kept them from asphyxiating. Two years later, Apollo 17 astronauts used duct tape to repair the fender of a damaged lunar rover.

243

Historically, it has been difficult for a pirate to convert to Christianity. They have a hard time giving up their booty.

244
TODAY'S QUOTE

"Keep your eyes wide open before marriage, half shut afterwards."

Ben Franklin

245
DID YOU KNOW?

The first Swiss Army Knife, designed by cutler Karl Elsener, featured two blades, a screw-driver, and a can opener. The world's first multi-tool was distributed to Swiss Army soldiers in 1891. Today's versions of the Swiss Army Knife sport such features as an altimeter, an alarm clock, a barometer, a pharmaceutical spatula, and a USB flash drive.

TODAY'S QUOTE

"There is no 'I' in team. And, for my friends on
eBay, there is no 'D' in refrigerator either."

Todd Hafer

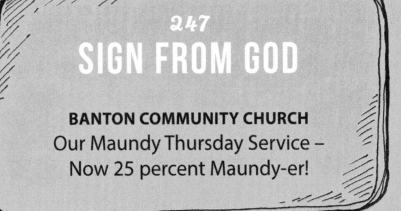

247

SIGN FROM GOD

BANTON COMMUNITY CHURCH
Our Maundy Thursday Service –
Now 25 percent Maundy-er!

DID YOU KNOW?

On a long hike, bike ride, or camping trip and you've forgotten your lip balm? Ear wax will get the job done, if you're brave enough to use it.

TODAY'S QUOTE

"Here's a question I wish more teen girls would ask themselves: 'Do these booty shorts make my dignity look smaller?'"

Jedd Hafer

DID YOU KNOW?

Mountain House, the maker of 33 varieties of freeze-dried meals, began as a supplier to the U.S. Military. Its 11-ounce Long Range Patrol rations, featuring cigarettes, gum, and 1,000-calorie entrees like chicken and rice or spaghetti with meat sauce, replaced the wet-packed C rations that were developed during World War II. Before long, the unused LRP meals began to show up at Army-surplus stores, where they were discovered by back-packers. Today's Mountain House meals, which no longer include cigarettes, have a shelf life of 30 years.

MAJOR LEAGUE BASEBALL'S ALL-TIME, ALL-RELIGION TEAM

CATCHER: Steve Christmas

1ST BASE: Jim Gentile

2ND BASE: Lave Cross

3RD BASE: Max Bishop

OUTFIELD: Bob Christian

OUTFIELD: Howie Nunn

OUTFIELD: Johnny Priest

DESIGNATED HITTER: Bris Lord

PITCHERS: Bill Parsons, Preacher Roe, and Adrian Devine

252
TODAY'S QUOTE

"I'm the kind of guy who can walk into an empty room and blend right in."

Todd Hafer

253
SPEAKING OF SPORTS . . .

"I'd give my right arm to be ambidextrous."

Yogi Berra

DID YOU KNOW?

The Nalgene Bottle, the wide-mouthed receptacle indispensable to outdoors people, was originally created to hold chemicals. In the mid-1970s, scientists at Nalgene, a New York manufacturer of plastic lab equipment, began sneaking various bottles out of company headquarters to use on camping trips. Then, company president Marsh Hyman gave a few bottles to his son, for use on Boy Scout outings. Before long, Hyman directed his company to promote the sturdy Nalgene bottles to the outdoor community. (The myth that a duct-tape-wrapped Nalgene bottle can survive being run over by a car is unconfirmed, as of the publication of this book.)

255
YOU KNOW YOU'RE A SPORTS FANATIC WHEN . . .

Your résumé includes your high bowling score, your golf handicap, and a history of your hamstring injuries.

256
TODAY'S QUOTE

"The other day, I walked into a General Store. The proprietor asked what I was looking for. I answered, 'Oh, nothing specific.'"

Constance Rivers

257
DID YOU KNOW?

Pu Yi became Emperor of China when he was only three years old. However, the Republican Revolution forced young Pu to abdicate his post – at the ripe old age of six.

258
TODAY'S QUOTE

"I have a spine of iron. It is rusty and does not want to bend."

Drew Cody

A SHOT AT LOVE

At age 15, sharp-shooting prodigy Annie Oakley defeated a professional marksman named Frank Butler in a shooting competition. But instead of resenting the young woman's victory, Butler fell in love with her. A year later, the duo married and Butler became his five-foot wife's assistant on the traveling Buffalo Bill's Wild West Show. Butler trusted his wife's skill so much that their act included Annie's shooting a dime out of her husband's hand – and a cigarette from his mouth. Annie, who learned to shoot at age eight, could also hit a playing card tossed into the air by Butler, at a distance of 90 feet. (Incidentally, in her later years, Annie served as a shooting instructor for the U.S. military during World War I.)

TODAY'S QUOTE

"I stopped believing in Santa Claus when I was six. Mother took me to see him in a department store, and he asked for my autograph."

Former child star, Shirley Temple

DID YOU KNOW?

Over the years, many couples have relied on the relationship and intimacy advice of Dr. Ruth Westheimer. But few know that before she found fame as an author and therapist, Westheimer was a trained sniper in the Israeli army.

262
TODAY'S QUOTE

"I can run the country or I can control [my daughter] Alice. I cannot do both."

President Theodore Roosevelt

263
DID YOU KNOW?

August Rodin worked slowly as both a sculptor and suitor. At age 23, he met and befriended a woman named Rose Beuret. However, it took him 53 years to get around to marrying Rose, when he was 76 and she was 73.

264
TODAY'S QUOTE

"Before I got married, I had six theories about bringing up children. Now I have six children, and no theories."

John Wilmot, Earl of Rochester

265
DID YOU KNOW?

If someone could design a race car that could run on methane, the daily flatulence of a single sheep could power that car for 25 miles.

266
YOU KNOW YOU'RE A SPORTS FANATIC WHEN . . .

You can't even look at a French baguette without wondering how far you could hit a baseball with it.

267
DID YOU KNOW?

Parachute cord (or paracord or P-cord) might be the world's most versatile survival tool. It can repair torn clothing, bind tent poles, or construct a webbing for a makeshift hammock. If you pull apart paracord's inner strands, you have fishing line, dental floss, or thread thin and strong enough to suture a wound. In 1977, space-shuttle Discovery astronauts used P-cord to repair damaged insulation on the Hubble Space Telescope.

268
YOU KNOW YOU'RE A SPORTS FANATIC WHEN . . .

You've used more duct tape on the grips of your tennis racket and golf clubs than you have doing household repairs.

269
TODAY'S QUOTE

"There's a difference between following Jesus . . . and following Jesus on Facebook, Twitter, and Instagram."

Todd Hafer

CHURCH BULLETIN BLOOPERS, SPORTS EDITION, VOLUME 2

Support our church youth soccer team, via the recycling fundraiser. We encourage you to haul your cans to church, whether they are big or small!

The Middle School volleyball team's trip to the Alligator Farm has been cancelled due to an outbreak of common sense.

Annual Youth Kickball Game cancelled due to the fact that it's not 1972.

This week's softball game will be hell at United Methodist Church.

THE REPURPOSING HALL OF FAME

Do you pride yourself on your ability to re-use, re-purpose, and recycle around the house or office?

Then you will applaud these companies for creatively recycling and reusing various materials:

- Patagonia uses plastic bottles to make fleece for new jackets.

- Alchemy Goods makes wallets out of old bicycle inner tubes.

- Kialoa Paddles makes blades out of diaper-manufacturing scraps.

- Manduka makes flip-flops out of old yoga mats.

272
YOU KNOW YOU'RE A SPORTS FANATIC WHEN . . .

You consider your bowling-team
shirt "business casual."

273
TODAY'S QUOTE

"Brilliance is like four-wheel drive: It enables
a person to get stuck in even more remote
places."

Garrison Keillor

DID YOU KNOW?

The spork first appeared in the dictionary in 1909 ("a spoon-shaped eating utensil with short tines at the front, and that is usually plastic"). It's been part of American lore ever since. During World War II, General Douglas MacArthur gave sporks to Japanese prisoners, to prevent them from attacking Allied soldiers with forks or chopsticks. This might not have been a sound decision. In 2008, a robber held up a bank in Alaska, armed only with a spork

from a nearby fried-chicken restaurant. Today, the spork has evolved from the traditional spoon with small fork tines added to its tip. A Swedish company called Light My Fire has reimagined the spork as a utensil with a spoon at one end and a fork at the other. The firm has sold more than 20 million of its "sporks" in 52 countries.

275
SPEAKING OF SPORTS . . .

"Baseball is like church. Many attend,
but few understand."

Wes Westrum

276
A GRAND COMEDY
DEBUT

Comedian Bernie Mac performed his first
stand-up routine at a church event when he
was only 8 years old. He earned quite a few
laughs, but his spot-on impersonation of his
grandparents also earned him a spanking.

TODAY'S QUOTE

"If God didn't want man to hunt, he wouldn't have given us plaid shirts."

Johnny Carson

EPIC WEST-FALIA

Despite being notoriously prone to breakdowns and expensive repairs, the Westfalia Volkswagen camper vans are beloved by road-trippers everywhere. The Westfalia prototype was created in 1951, when the automotive contractor Westfalia-Werke retrofitted a Volkswagen camper for a British army officer who wanted to transform his transit van into a mobile home. The idea worked so well that

Westfalia went into full production mode, adding features like a kitchen, all-wheel drive, and a pop-top. Thousands of Westfalias were sold until production ceased in 2001. Since then, a cottage industry of repair and refurbishment shops has sprung up.

Westfalia breakdowns are frequent, and repairs are expensive. A blown head gasket runs about $3,000. Nonetheless, rebuilt Westfalias sell for more than $90,000, and these camper vans are one of the most popular subjects on websites like Instagram.

279
SPEAKING OF SPORTS . . .

"Me shooting 40 percent from the foul line is just God's way to say nobody's perfect."

NBA legend Shaquille O'Neal (who once went 0 for 11 from the line in one game)

280
DID YOU KNOW?

Franz Liszt established himself as a virtuoso concert pianist by the time he was 12. He performed throughout Europe, often having his hair and clothing pulled from his person by adoring female fans. He received so many requests for a lock of his hair, via the mail, that he bought a dog and began snipping off its hair to send to his many female admirers.

TODAY'S QUOTE

"I love Twitter. I could go on and on about how great it is. I just hope I don't exceed my . . ."

Jedd Hafer

TODAY'S QUOTE

"Artists create beauty. Judges settle disputes. Spiritual leaders inspire hope. Journalists uncover truth. Police officers keep peace. Doctors and nurses save lives. We teachers do all of the above – plus handle lunch and playground duty!"

Marcia Edwards

DID YOU KNOW?

Many Americans are ailurophiles. That is, they really, really love their cats. In the United States, 67 percent of the 90 million cats get to sleep in bed with their owners Almost 40 percent of cats receive at least one Christmas present. All told, American cat owners spend about a thousand dollars a year on each of their furry friends.

YOU KNOW YOU'RE A SPORTS FANATIC WHEN . . .

You follow the Phillie Phanatic on Twitter.

TODAY'S QUOTE

"My weaknesses have always been
food and men, in that order."

Dolly Parton

DID YOU KNOW?

A 19-year-old, 115-pound college student
named Kate Stelneck became the first person
to eat the Ye Old 96er Burger at Denny's Beer
Barrel Pub in Clearfield, PA. Consuming the
six-pound burger (and its five pounds of con-
diments) took Kate two hours and 54 minutes,
just under the challenge's three-hour time
limit.

289
SOMETHING TO PONDER

If you pull a fly's wings off,
can you still call it a fly?

290
TODAY'S QUOTE

"In this bad economy, the only difference
between me and a pigeon is that a pigeon can
still make a deposit on a new hunting rifle."

Tim Hanson

DID YOU KNOW?

At the age of 78, Dale Davis rolled a perfect 300 in a bowling league playoff game. And Mr. Davis is legally blind. The Iowa bowler has no vision in his left eye and only very blurry vision from the corner of his right eye – just enough to allow him to line up a shot in a bowling lane.

DID YOU KNOW?

For centuries, people (especially men) have ingested various animal, vegetable, and mineral concoctions in search of the ultimate love potion.

A current fad is rhino horn, which you might find on the shelves of your local drug store or nutrition supplement shop. However, while rhinos are large and powerful, ingesting their horns is an act of futility. A rhino's horn is really just a dense, hard-packed compound of hair and keratin – the stuff your fingernails are made of. Thus, a guy would do just as well to chew his hair and bite his fingernails. The effect on the libido is the same – and you'll help save the rhino, which is endangered.

293

The Reverend Del Hafer once portrayed the prophet Isaiah in a church Christmas pageant. The bathrobe he chose as part of his costume granted some of the parishioners' wish to "see more of our pastor."

294
SPEAKING OF SPORTS . . .

"It took me 17 years to get 3,000 hits in baseball. I did it in one afternoon on the golf course."

Hammerin' Hank Aaron

295
TODAY'S QUOTE

"Adam invented the joke. One day, Eve asked him, 'Adam, do you love me?' He shrugged his bare shoulders and replied, 'Who else?'"

Drew Cody

296

DID YOU KNOW?

That adage about a dog's mouth being
cleaner than a human's is simply not true.
Yes, the human mouth harbors 37 types of
bacteria, but a dog's mouth sports 53 varieties.
So the next time you want to show your dog
some love, try a warm hug, a tummy rub, or
a game of fetch.

297

TODAY'S QUOTE

"They say women love a man in uniform.
It's true. The uniform sends a clear message:
He has a job."

Mimi Gonzalez

THE NATIONAL BASKETBALL ASSOCIATION'S ALL-SECOND-CAREER TEAM

G Bill Bradley
(U.S. Senator–as well as author
and presidential candidate)

G Chuck Conners
(actor–"The Rifleman")

C Tom McMillan
(U.S. Congressman)

F Wayman Tisdale
(jazz musician)

F Mark Hendrickson
(Major League Baseball player)

(Honorable Mention: F. Jerry Lucas–
author and memory expert)

YOU HAVE ZIP!

Somewhere in your closet –perhaps on your body right now – you sport the letters YKK. YKK stands for Yoshida Kogyo Kabushikikaisha, an 81-year-old Japanese zipper company. To maintain YKK's strict standards, the company keeps every stage of zipper-making in-house. They smelt the brass, forge the zipper teeth, and spin the thread. In Japan, YKK even makes the packaging the zippers are shipped in. YKK produces more than 1 million miles of zippers every year. They are used in everything from jeans to fanny packs to expedition tents.

300
TODAY'S QUOTE

"If we didn't have teachers, no one would know when to come back from recess – or how to spell!"

Olivia Kent, age 8

301
"TOLD YOU TV WATCHING WAS BAD FOR YOU!"

Manchester City goalkeeper David Seaman probably thought he got his bad luck out of the way when he tore up his shoulder while reeling in a prize carp on a fishing trip.

But he was wrong. A short while later, Seaman broke his hand – while reaching for his TV remote.

DID YOU KNOW?

In 1988, a cyclist and paramedic named Michael Eidson competed in a grueling race called the Hotter 'N Hell Hundred in Wichita Falls, TX. To help hydrate during the long ride, Eidson fashioned a mobile drinking device from an IV bag, which he placed in a tube sock. He slid the sock into his pocket, then clipped the IV bag's hose to his jersey with a clothespin. As he sipped from the contraption during the race, many other riders took note. After the race, he decided to mass-produce his device, which he dubbed the ThermoBak. Later, he changed the name to CamelBak, which soon became indispensable for endurance athletes . . . and the U.S. military.

303
YOU KNOW YOU'RE A SPORTS FANATIC WHEN . . .

You know where your
fishing license is, but not
your marriage license.

304
TODAY'S QUOTE

"The simplest toy, one which even the youngest child can operate, is called a grandparent."

Sam Evensong

A THEOLOGIAN'S TAKE ON GOLF . . .

"Golf is an expensive way of playing marbles."

G.K. Chesterton

TODAY'S QUOTE

"Of course I know the ages of all my grand-children! The doctor is seven, the theoretical physicist is five, the NFL quarterback is two, and the CEO is seven months old."

H. J. Springston

306

The Reverend Del Hafer could tailor a message
to any audience. He once told a pack of Boy
Scouts, "As Saint Paul would tell you, 'When
I was a Cub Scout, I spoke and thought as a
Cub Scout, but when I became a Webelo, I put
away Cub Scout things.'"

THE HIPPOPOTAMUS OF LOVE?

The Steve Miller Band's 1973 hit "The Joker" features one of the most misquoted lyrics in pop music. Some people swear that Miller sings about "the hippopotamus of love" – raising the question, "What, precisely, is the hippopotamus of love?"

Actually, the lyric is "the pompatus of love." This provides little clarification, as there is no such word as pompatus.

What Miller and company were aiming for, most likely, was "puppetutes of love." A puppetute is a paper-doll fantasy figure that can fulfill a man's romantic wishes. The 1954 Medallions song "The Letter" refers to a puppetute. Apparently, Miller tried to borrow this line for his song, but he got confused. Perhaps that's why some people call him "The Space Cowboy."

YOU KNOW YOU'RE A SPORTS FANATIC WHEN . . .

You execute holds on your dog while watching televised mixed-martial arts.

TODAY'S QUOTE

"As the skunk philosopher once said, 'I stink, therefore I am.'"

Drew Cody

DID YOU KNOW?

Near midnight on November 29 (the day before Saint Andrew's Day), it is traditional for young Scottish women to petition Saint Andrew for a husband.

To receive a sign that the saint has heard her, a woman can do one of two things:

Throw a shoe at a door in her home. If the toe of the shoe points toward the exit, that's a sign that the young woman will marry and leave her home within a year.

Peel a whole apple rind and toss it over her shoulder. If the rind forms a letter of the alphabet, it will be the first initial of her future groom.

312
YOU KNOW YOU'RE A SPORTS FANATIC WHEN . . .

You're secretly disappointed that the *Sports Illustrated* swimsuit issue doesn't have more stories and photos of "real sports."

314
TODAY'S QUOTE

"Have you tried the new Hafer Brothers After Shave? It comes in regular and unscented!"

Jedd and Todd Hafer

THE SECRET OF GILL-MAN

While creating the 1954 movie Creature from the Black Lagoon, filmmakers encountered a problem with Gill-Man, the prehistoric Amazon creature at the center of the action. They could not devise a way to incorporate air tanks into Gill-Man's costume – without making things obvious to the audience. Eventually, they found a solution. They hired Olympic swimmer Ricou Browning to don Gill-Man's costume for all underwater scenes. Browning could hold his breath for up to four minutes, feeding the illusion that the famed "creature" could, in fact, breathe underwater through his gills.

A STUNT WITH A CATCH

During a publicity stunt in 1917, former big-league catcher Wilbert Robinson prepared himself to receive what he thought was a baseball, thrown from a biplane. What actually came Robinson's way was a grapefruit, which exploded on impact with his glove. Robinson mistook the citrus juice for his own blood and fell to the ground, screaming that he was going to die.

316

TODAY'S QUOTE

"I'm the president of the United States, and I'm not going to eat any more broccoli!"

President George H. W. Bush

318

A potluck tip: When choosing a brownie or slice of cake, go for a corner piece. You get more frosting that way, and even an inept cook cannot mess up frosting.

SPEAKING OF SPORTS . . .

"Golf is a good walk spoiled."

Mark Twain

DID YOU KNOW?

It's said that there is a woman for every man, but in the emirate of Qatar, it's simply not true. Qatar has the worst male-to-female ratio (from a guy's perspective) of any country in the world. There are 2.36 eligible men for every woman, which puts Qatar well ahead of second-place Kuwait, with its 1.77 male-to-female ratio.

320
"COULD YOU PLEASE REPEAT THAT?"

At the age of 72, golfer Suzan Toft aced the 116-yard par 3 hole at England's Trentham course. A TV crew heard about the feat and, after arriving on the scene, jokingly, asked Toft if she could repeat it. She grabbed her 5-wood and sank the tee shot again.

321
SPEAKING OF SPORTS . . .

"Left hand, right hand, it doesn't matter. I'm amphibious."

Basketball player Charles Shackleford

322
TODAY'S QUOTE

"What kind of line do I use when I go fishing? Usually, 'I am only doing this to save money on our food budget, Honey.'"

Rich Tennant

323
REMINISCING

Dad taught us to swim the old-fashioned way. He took us down to the river and threw us in. And we learned to swim that very day. Although for a while, we were not sure we'd ever get out of that gunny sack.

Jedd and Todd Hafer

324
YOU KNOW YOU'RE A SPORTS FANATIC WHEN . . .

Your marriage license is signed by the commissioner of Major League Baseball.

325
TODAY'S QUOTE

"I have a friend who is a psychiatrist for flies. He helps them get in touch with their inner maggots."

George House

326
"THIS ONE'S FOR YOU, MOM"

Cleveland pitcher Bob Feller never forgot May 14, 1939. In the third inning, Chicago's Marvin Owen swung at a Feller pitch, fouling it into the first-base stands. It hit a female spectator in the face, causing her to be hospitalized for several days with painful (but non-critical) injuries. The victim? Feller's mother, who was in the stands as a guest of honor, on Mother's Day.

THE BIG LOUD CICADA DATE

Resting up before a big date is a good idea. But the cicada takes this principle to the extreme. Some species hibernate underground for up to 17 years before finally waking up and emerging to mate. The male cicada plays a love song to his potential mate, using a pair of ribbed membranes on his abdomen. Some cicadas sing their love songs at 120 decibels, the pain threshold for the human ear. Others sing in a pitch so high that it's beyond the range of human hearing.

Once a male wins a female's heart through song, the two mate. The female lays her eggs. Then Mr. and Mrs. Cicada die. But in another 17 years or so, their children will emerge to carry on the family name.

TODAY'S QUOTE

"Nothing makes a fish bigger
than almost being caught."

Andrew DeStefano

DID YOU KNOW?

Assigned to cover the 1933 Indy 500 auto race, a Denver sports-writer called his newspaper and promised, "Will overhead winner" – meaning he would send the winner's name via the overhead telegraph wires when the race was complete. His editor, unfortunately, misunderstood, thinking that a driver named Will Overhead had captured the race. The headline the next morning in the World Independent newspaper read: "Overhead Wins Indianapolis Race."

330
SPEAKING OF SPORTS . . .

"Cool Papa Bell was so fast he could get out of bed, turn out the lights across the room, and be back in bed, under the covers, before the lights went out."

Josh Gibson

331
TODAY'S QUOTE

"If you get a chance, come see us perform live. It's like getting a hug from Venus de Milo."

Jedd and Todd Hafer

BREAK A LEG, MR. AND MRS. FRANKENSTEIN

Elsa Lanchester, a five-feet, four-inch actress, played the title role in the 1935 film *The Bride of Frankenstein*. To see eye to eye with her monstrous spouse, played by Boris Karloff, Lanchester spent the entire film trussed to a pair of stilts, which made her seven feet tall. Ms. Lanchester proved quite nimble on her stilts.

Karloff, who wore lifts in his shoes to boost his height, was not so lucky. During the filming of one scene, he stumbled into a well and broke his leg.

333
TODAY'S QUOTE

"It's not that chocolates are a substitute for love. Love is a substitute for chocolate. Chocolate is, let's face it, for more reliable than a man."

Miranda Ingram

335
YOU KNOW YOU'RE A SPORTS FANATIC WHEN . . .

You think "The Nutcracker" is the nickname of a linebacker for the Green Bay Packers.

MORE NOTABLE SPORTS CAREER CHANGES

Bert Jones–an NFL quarterback turned lumber mill operator

Byron White–an NFL halfback turned Supreme Court Justice

Rich Franklin–math teacher turned world-champion mixed-martial-arts fighter

Billy Cannon–pro football halfback turned orthodontist

TODAY'S QUOTE

"Yes, I loved her as a man loves a woman, and she loved me. When that pigeon died, something went out of my life. I knew my life's work was over."

Nikola Tesla, Scientist
(AND A GUY REALLY, REALLY FOND OF HIS PET PIGEON)

SPEAKING OF SPORTS . . .

"I owe a lot to my parents, especially my mother and father."

Golfer Greg Norman

338
DID YOU KNOW?

A diamond isn't necessarily forever, despite what the song says. Diamonds are composed of pure carbon and are renowned for being one of the hardest and most durable substances known to humanity.

However, even a diamond will sublime at high temperatures. At 3,500 degrees Celsius, a diamond will turn directly from a solid to a gas.

YOU KNOW YOU'RE A SPORTS FANATIC WHEN . . .

Your home-security system is a 9-iron
propped against your nightstand

TODAY'S QUOTE

"Would you like to buy some clichés?
They're only a dime a dozen."

Drew Cody

342
HEAD OF ADVERTISING

A Nebraska-based web designer named Andrew Fisher used eBay to auction his forehead as advertising space. While some scoffed at the idea, the 20-year-old Fisher received $37,375 to display the logo for a snoring remedy, for the duration of 30 days.

343
YOU KNOW YOU'RE A SPORTS FANATIC WHEN . . .

You win at Scrabble by busting out "Krzyzewski."

344

TODAY'S QUOTE

"Even if you've fished for three hours and gotten nothing but a sunburn and a backache . . . you're still better off than the worm!"

Marv Edwards

345

DID YOU KNOW?

During an average NASCAR race at Talladega, about 12,000 pounds of hot dogs are served. (If those dogs were laid end to end, they would circle the 2.66-mile track, with another .14 miles worth of hot dogs to spare.)

346
SIGNS YOU MIGHT NEED COUNSELING FOR YOUR "ENERGY DRINK PROBLEM"

You gargle with Red Bull-flavored mouthwash.

You can be found in the workplace break room playing Ping Pong.Without an opponent.

You named your cats Caffeine, Guarana, and Taurine.

At church, you finish reciting "The Lord's Prayer" fifteen seconds before everyone else.

You haven't blinked since 1998.

347
DO THE MATH!

At the age of 49, Jeanette Roberts, a 35-handicapper, carded an amazing three aces in five rounds at the Granite Bay Golf Club. A mathematician projected that, on the average, a golfer would have to hit a tee shot on a par-3 hole every minute of every hour of every day—for 5,700 years to equal Roberts's feat.

348
TODAY'S QUOTE

"You know you've been married a long time when you start turning off the lights for economic reasons rather than romantic ones."

H. J. Springston

349

YOU KNOW YOU'RE A SPORTS FANATIC WHEN . . .

You refer to birth-control pills as
the "prevent defense."

350

SPEAKING OF SPORTS . . .

"Baseball players are smarter than football
players. How often do you see a baseball team
penalized for too many men on the field?"

Jim Bouton

TODAY'S QUOTE

"Whenever I see a crutch lying on the side of the road, I like to think a miracle happened."

Jedd Hafer

A KISS IS NOT JUST A KISS, AT LEAST NOT IN GERMANY

The English language has its share of synonyms for a kiss: smooch, smack, and peck, just to name a few. But the German language has more than 30 words for the act of kissing. And just to show their fluency on the subject, the Germans have a word – nachkuss – for any kisses yet to be named.

353

TODAY'S QUOTE

"A man knows when he is growing old,
because he begins to look like his father."

Gabriel Garcia Marquez

354

YOU KNOW YOU'RE A SPORTS FANATIC WHEN . . .

You call your local clergyperson "coach."

TODAY'S QUOTE

"This might be the most important lesson I've learned in life: Never pick a fight with your kids' teacher, Little League coach, or the woman they call Mom!"

H. J. Springston

SPEAKING OF SPORTS . . .

"I've never seen anyone on the disabled list with pulled fat."

Portly baseball pitcher, Rod Beck

TODAY'S QUOTE

"I never hated a man enough to give
him his diamonds back."

Zsa Zsa Gabor

358

DID YOU KNOW?

Hundreds of years ago, chocolate's reputation
as a love enhancer raised the ire of organized
religion. In the 17th century, theologian Jo-
hannes Franciscus condemned chocolate
as an "inflamer of passions." He command-
ed monks to abstain from drinking any co-
coa-based beverage, and he demanded that
chocolate, in all its dark forms, be banned from
all monasteries and other holy places.

TODAY'S QUOTE

"There are few things more satisfying in life than seeing your children have teenagers of their own."

Dave Barry

SPEAKING OF SPORTS . . .

"They both – bikinis and statistics – show a lot, but not everything."

Toby Harrah, MLB infielder

CHECK, MATE!

In the year 1213, King Ferrand of Portugal was captured and imprisoned by the Turks. The king's captors demanded a ransom for his release. His wife, Queen Jeanne, refused to pay up. She let her spouse languish for 13 years.

The reason? Shortly before the Turks invaded, the king and queen engaged in a spirited game of chess. The queen was victorious, and the sore-loser king punched his wife in the nose.

The queen recovered and had many years to enjoy the ultimate check-mate.

A BRIEF AND DIZZYING EXCHANGE

British news reporter (to baseball player Dizzy Dean): "Mr. Dean, don't you know the king's English?"

Dizzy Dean (after a moment's reflection): "Sure I do, and so is the Queen!"

TODAY'S QUOTE

"We wanted to include a picture of a beautiful wheat field in this book, but the photo was too grainy."

Jedd and Todd Hafer

364
BREAKING DOWN BASEBALL

"A baseball game is simply a nervous breakdown divided into nine innings."

Earl Wilson

365
ROAMING CHARGES OF THE HEART

A 24-year-old Denmark man found himself facing jail time for fraud, because he was unable to pay a $117,000 phone bill for calls to his sweetheart in India. The lovelorn Dane made a love connection with a young woman in the city of Madras. And what a connection it was! One of the calls stretched beyond 21 hours.

DID YOU KNOW?

Outfielder Carlos May is, unofficially, the only pro athlete to wear his birthday on his uniform. He was born on May 17 – which is exactly what was stitched on the back of his jersey.

TODAY'S QUOTE

"This past Christmas, I saw a pine tree walk into a barber shop and say, 'I'd like a trim, please.'"

George House

369
REMINISCING

Our dad was a pastor, and you never wanted to be late for one of his church services. You'd try to slide into a back pew, and he'd point at you and say, "Welcome! Can I get you anything – like a watch!?"

Jedd and Todd Hafer

370
SPEAKING OF SPORTS . . .

"Trying to sneak a fastball past Hank Aaron is like trying to sneak sunrise past a rooster."

Joe Adcock

elevate
publishing

DELIVERING TRANSFORMATIVE MESSAGES
TO THE WORLD

Visit www.elevatepub.com for our latest offerings.

NO TREES WERE HARMED IN THE MAKING OF THIS BOOK.

OK, so a few did need to make the ultimate sacrifice.

In order to steward our environment, we are partnered with *Plant With Purpose*, to plant a tree for every tree that paid the price for the printing of this book.

To learn more, visit wwwelevatepub.com/about

PLANT W TH PURPOSE | WWW.PLANTWITHPURPOSE.ORG

CPSIA information can be obtained
at www.ICGtesting.com
Printed in the USA
BVOW10*0859020616

450488BV00010B/38/P